AMAZING Teachers & YOU!

To my loves, Robert, April, and Richard:
You have taught me so much about embracing
the creative spirit and belief in oneself!
—G. O. S.

To my mother, for always being the best teacher.

—A. L.

This is a work of fiction. Names, characters, places, and incidents either are the product of the author's imagination or are used fictitiously. Any resemblance to actual persons, living or dead, events, or locales is entirely coincidental.

First Edition, April 2021

Book design by Elynn Cohen

ISBN 978-1-7370619-0-8 (paperback)
ISBN 978-1-7370619-1-5 (hardcover)
ISBN 978-1-7370619-2-2 (ebook)

www.childresilience.com

AMAZING Teachers & YOU!

Geraldine V. Oades-Sese, PH.D.
illustrated by Arthur Lin

Teachers are amazing people.
They nurture your mind and guide your way,

Walk by your side
and **inspire!**

C
D
E
F

Teachers can turn the ordinary into the **extraordinary**.

They help you travel to faraway lands,
tread among the **dinosaurs**,

Go on wild **safaris** and dig for **buried treasure**!

But when you get lost along the way,

PERSIST!

And remember. . .

Pause and take a deep breath,
Your teacher is there for you.
Tell them how you feel and why,
And they will help you through.

Teachers encourage you to
imagine and create.
They drive you to invent a flying school,
pretend to sail the seven seas,

Erect a puppet theater and paint
an original masterpiece!

Teachers show you how to **build and measure**. They challenge you to climb the highest hills, raise the tallest buildings, construct the strongest bridges

and race to **outer space**.

But when things don't go as planned
and instead break and fall,
have PATIENCE!
Be FLEXIBLE!

And remember. . .

Pause and take a deep breath,
Your teacher is there for you.
Tell them how you feel and why,
And they will help you through.

Teachers help bring out the **superhero** in you!

They push you to **tame** that angry lion,
surf a tidal wave,
Lift a gazillion pound weight and **face**
those scary monsters!

But when you feel **frustrated**
or overwhelmed, don't hit or shout!

Instead, speak **softly** and **calmly.**
Use **kind words** and **gentle hands.**

And when your feelings become too big to handle,
be **BRAVE** and **ASK for HELP**!

And remember. . .

Pause and take a deep breath,
Your teacher is there for you.
Tell them how you feel and why,
And they will help you through.

One day, you will remember those **amazing teachers**—
And how they nurtured and guided you!

Someday it will be **your turn** to share important lessons and inspire someone, too!

1x2 =

About the Author and Illustrator

Geraldine V. Oades-Sese, Ph.D. ("Dr. Gerry"), is a licensed child psychologist in New Jersey. Before private practice, she was the Associate Director and Associate Professor at the Institute for the Study of Child Development at Rutgers University RWJ Medical School, and a faculty member at the Rutgers Graduate School of Applied and Professional Psychology. She served as an advisor to Sesame Workshop and WNET Thirteen PBS Kids. Building resilience in children is the focus of her research and publications. This is her first picture book. She is an avid birder, Sherlockian, and enjoys her flower garden.

Arthur Lin is a San Francisco native who always finds inspiration through his childhood. He has illustrated multiple books to his credit and always remembered the invaluable advice his teachers have given him over the years. He is currently being represented by Shannon Associates.

Search and Find: Can you find the Dr. Gerry dolls in the story?